12/25/2015
Addison —
Look real close — enjoy
the adventure.

Love, Auntie Marlene

Can You Find It,Too?

Can You Find It, Too?

Judith Cressy

The Metropolitan Museum of Art

Abrams Books for Young Readers
New York

For copyrighted material, all rights are reserved. Photographs were in most cases provided by the owners of the works and are published with their permission; their courtesy is gratefully acknowledged. Additional credits follow:

Front cover: GG Inv. No. 1017; back cover: Gift of Frederic H. Hatch, 1926 26.97; title page: The Edward W. C. Arnold Collection of New York Prints, Maps, and Pictures, Bequest of Edward W. C. Arnold, 1954 54.90.169; pages 6–7: The Friedsam Collection, Bequest of Michael Friedsam, 1931 32.100.69; pages 10–11: Reproduced with the permission of Carol Lowry; page 12: Rogers Fund, 1923 23.2.84; page 13: Courtesy of the J. Paul Getty Museum 85.PB.117; pages 14–15: Gift of Jeffrey Paley, 1974 1974.221; pages 16–17: Photo by Arnandet; Image © Réunion des Musées Nationaux / Art Resource, N.Y. INV 2898 ART162023; pages 18–19: Purchase, The Dillon Fund Gift, 1988 1988.350 a-d; page 20: Purchase, Edward C. Moore Jr. Gift, 1928 28.63.3; pages 22–23: Photo by Lyle Peterzell; Samuel H. Kress Collection 1952.2.19; pages 24–25: Photo by Antonio Quattrone; pages 26–27: GG Inv. No. 1017; pages 28–29: Image © Réunion des Musées Nationaux / Art Resource, N.Y. INV 3699 ART147623; page 30: © 2004 Artists Rights Society (ARS), New York / VEGAP, Madrid Photo by David Heald; Gift, Royal S. Marks in memory of Gertrude Marks and Herbert F. Gower Jr., 1987 88.3568; page 31: Edith C. Blum Fund, 1986 1986.108; pages 32–33: NG846 Bought with the Peel collection, 1871; pages 34–35: Gift of Mrs. Vincent Astor, 1978 1978.493

Published in 2004 by The Metropolitan Museum of Art, New York, and Harry N. Abrams, Incorporated, New York
Copyright © 2004 by The Metropolitan Museum of Art

First Edition
Printed in China
16 15 14 13 12 11 10 09 08 07   10 9 8 7 6

Produced by the Department of Special Publications, The Metropolitan Museum of Art:
Robie Rogge, Publishing Manager; Jessica Schulte, Project Editor; Gillian Moran, Production Associate.
Photography by The Metropolitan Museum of Art Photograph Studio, unless otherwise noted.

Designed by Miriam Berman

Visit the Museum's Web site: www.metmuseum.org

Library of Congress Cataloging-in-Publication Data
Cressy, Judith.
   Can you find it, too? / Judith Cressy.
      p. cm.
ISBN 1-58839-053-5 (MMA)—ISBN 0-8109-5046-4 (Abrams)
1. Art appreciation—Juvenile literature. I. Title.

N7440.C78 2004
750'.1'1—dc22
                    2004004840

HNA
harry n. abrams, inc.
a subsidiary of La Martinière Groupe
115 West 18th Street
New York, NY 10011
www.hnabooks.com

In this painting of
an old-fashioned hotel
can you find

12

yellow wheels

6

birdhouses

2

women with red skirts

1

man in a tree

1

hat with a long black streamer

1

flag with 11 stars

2

horse-and-carriages without drivers

2

hanging lanterns

The Claremont (detail)
Unknown artist, American, circa 1855
Oil on canvas
The Metropolitan Museum of Art, New York

We started playing "Can You Find It?" in the galleries of The Metropolitan Museum of Art in New York, looking at paintings and finding details that we had never noticed before. It's a satisfying game, in part for the sheer fun of discovery, but also because in the process of looking, you learn so much about the paintings. It's amazing what you will find when you look very closely at art.

After beginning our discoveries together in *Can You Find It?*, we expanded our search internationally to create *Can You Find It, Too?* On these pages, paintings from the Metropolitan Museum are joined by selections from three other American museums: the J. Paul Getty Museum in Los Angeles, the Solomon R. Guggenheim Museum in New York City, and the National Gallery of Art in Washington, D.C.—and from seven European collections—the Alte Pinakothek in Munich, the Arts Council Collection and the National Gallery of Art in London, the Kunsthistorisches Museum in Vienna, the Louvre in Paris, the Medici-Riccardi Palace in Florence, and the Prado in Madrid. When you play "Can You Find It?," you soon discover surprises in paintings everywhere.

You can play the "Can You Find It?" game in this book or whenever you visit a museum. The rules are simple: Just find some details you can count, then challenge someone else to find them. The fun is in the looking.

—Judith Cressy

In this painting of
the story of Joseph
can you find

6

camels

1

herd of cows

2

cherubs

1

man in a red cap

4

boats

1

sheaf of wheat

1

shoulder with a lion's head

1

woman

The Story of Joseph (detail)
Biagio di Antonio, Italian (Florentine),
active by 1472, died 1516
Cassone panel; tempera on wood
The Metropolitan Museum of Art, New York

GVSEPPO

GVSEPPO · FARAGON

SONGO · DIFARAGONE

8

In this painting of
many scenes
can you find

1

nest of baby birds

1

hourglass

1

peacock

1

stormy sea

1

pair of porcupines

1

bird with its beak in a bottle

&

some playing cards

&

the artist's signature in worms

The Four Continents: Europe
Jan van Kessel, Flemish, 1626–1679
Painting with 17 panels, oil on copper
Alte Pinakothek, Munich

In this painting of
a crowded beach
can you find

4

baby carriages

2

open umbrellas

1

shovel in hand

2

boys on their backs

1

dog on a leash

1

trio of cyclists

1

signpost

2

kings of the hill

July, the Seaside
L. S. Lowry, British, 1887–1976
Oil on canvas
Arts Council Collection, Hayward Gallery, London

In this painting from **ancient Egypt** can you find

1
hare

3
cobras

1
falcon

4
beards

10
ears

7
hands

22
eyes

30
feet

Horemhab Offering Wine to Anubis
Unknown artist, Egyptian,
Dynasty 18, circa 1323–1295 B.C.
Watercolor facsimile by Lancelot Crane
The Metropolitan Museum of Art, New York

In this painting of **astronomers** can you find

1 bull's head

2 people writing

2 yellow feet

2 winged women

4 people pointing to the sky

1 bridge

2 flaming hats

3 obelisks

Dionysius the Areopagite Converting the Pagan Philosophers
Antoine Caron, French, 1520–1600
Oil on panel
The J. Paul Getty Museum, Los Angeles

In this painting from
India
can you find

1

musical horse

3

pinky rings

1

lotus flower

1

bull

1

flame

1

golden eye

3

mustaches

3

drummers

Vishnu as Varaha, the Cosmic Boar, Slays a Demon General
Unknown artist, Indian, Punjab Hills, Guler, circa 1800
Probably from a Mahabharata manuscript;
ink and color on paper
The Metropolitan Museum of Art, New York

In this painting of
**a triumphal
procession**
can you find

1

golden bull

6

snakes

2

goat heads

1

horseshoe

8

jingle bells

4

wings

1

lyre

1

golden ring

**The Entrance of Alexander into Babylon
or The Triumph of Alexander** (detail)
Charles Le Brun, French, 1619–1690
Oil on canvas
Louvre Museum, Paris

In this painting of
a Chinese city
can you find

1

man trying on boots

1

woman with a child

1

white beard

1

man carrying a
flowering branch

3

teapots

1

fish

4

horses

1

orange chair

**The Qianlong Emperor's
Southern Inspection Tour,
Scroll Six: Entering Suzhou
Along the Grand Canal** (detail)
Xu Yang, Chinese, active circa 1750–after 1776
Handscroll; ink and color on silk
The Metropolitan Museum of Art, New York

In this painting of
an Indian battle
can you find

2

sets of drums

2

elephants

17

horses

2

golden crowns

9

shields

3

men with bows

1

green boot

4

spears

Krishna and Balarama Fight the Enemy
Unknown artist, Indian, Mughal period, circa 1590-95
Leaf from a dispersed manuscript of the
Harivamsa (The Legend of Hari [Krishna]);
ink, color, and gold on paper
The Metropolitan Museum of Art, New York

In this painting of

people surrounding a hay wagon

can you find

2

fish

1

peacock feather

4

babies

2

ladders

1

owl

5

jugs

1

heart

1

man growing branches

The Haywain or Path of Life
Hieronymus Bosch,
Netherlandish, 1450–1516
Central panel of a triptych; oil on wood
Museo del Prado, Madrid

In this painting of

a fantastic landscape

can you find

1

owl

1

key

6

fish

1

funnel

2

boats

1

guitar

2

bells

1

man on fire

The Temptation of Saint Anthony
Follower of Pieter Bruegel the Elder,
Netherlandish, circa 1525–1569
Oil on panel
National Gallery of Art, Washington, D.C.

In this painting of
a grand procession
can you find

5

dogs

1

hat in hand

8

birds

1

pair of red-and-white legs

1

rabbit

1

forehead star

1

hat with writing on the rim

9

mustached men

Procession of the Young King
Benozzo Gozzoli (Benozzo di Lese di Sandro),
Italian (Florentine), 1420–1497
Tempera on plaster
Medici-Riccardi Palace, Florence

25

In this painting of
children playing
can you find

1

mask

1

wooden flute

2

red purses

2

boys on stilts

1

birdhouse

2

cone-shaped hats

1

flower basket

1

woman balancing
a broom

Children at Play (detail)
Pieter Bruegel the Elder, Netherlandish,
circa 1525–1569
Oil on wood
Kunsthistorisches Museum, Vienna

In this painting of
a coronation
can you find

1

hand without an arm

2

beards

1

golden pitcher

1

hat in hand

1

golden eagle

5

winged heads

1

angel

1

sword in hand

**Coronation of Emperor Napoléon and Josephine
at Notre Dame on December 2, 1804** (detail)
Jacques-Louis David, French, 1748–1825
Oil on canvas
Louvre Museum, Paris

In this painting of
a flat city
can you find

1

star

1

clock

1

house

1

apartment building

1

arrow

1

blimp

1

pulley

&

the number 140

Constructive Composition
Joaquín Torres-García, Uruguayan, 1874–1949
Oil on canvas
Solomon R. Guggenheim Museum, New York

In this painting of
a potter at work
can you find

1

sponge

1

funnel

9

spouts

1

piece of masking tape

1

loose-leaf notebook

1

spray can

1

pot of brushes

&

the number 129

Jeff Kleckner at Work
Dana Van Horn, American, born 1950
Oil on canvas
The Metropolitan Museum of Art, New York

31

In this painting of
an alchemist at work
can you find

1

pair of spectacles

1

hourglass

4

funnels

1

drill

1

broken plate

1

handwritten note

2

baskets

&

the artist's signature

An Alchemist (detail)
Adriaen van Ostade, Dutch, 1610–1685
Oil on wood
National Gallery, London

In this painting of
a French harbor
can you find

5

dogs

3

flags

1

large white bird

1

man with bare feet

2

anchors

1

guitar case

1

waterspout

&

the number 40

The Outer Harbor of Brest (detail)
Louis Nicholas van Blarenberghe, French, 1716–1794
Oil on canvas
The Metropolitan Museum of Art, New York

an old-fashioned hotel title page

- 12 yellow wheels
- 6 birdhouses
- 2 women with red skirts
- 1 man in a tree
- 1 hat with a long black streamer
- 1 flag with 11 stars
- 2 horse-and-carriages without drivers
- 2 hanging lanterns

The Claremont, unknown artist

Tradition has it that this painting was made in about 1855 by a self-taught itinerant artist in return for hospitality at the Claremont. The big red building was a private house before it became a popular inn and restaurant in the middle of the nineteenth century. Although the building no longer exists, it was located just outside New York City where it had spectacular views of the Hudson River.

The Metropolitan Museum of Art, New York

the story of Joseph pages 6-7

- 6 camels
- 1 herd of cows
- 2 cherubs
- 1 man in a red cap
- 4 boats
- 1 sheaf of wheat
- 1 shoulder with a lion's head
- 1 woman

The Story of Joseph, Biagio di Antonio

In Renaissance Italy, the traditional wooden storage chest, or *cassone,* was decorated with colorful scenes. This cassone panel depicts the story of Joseph from the Book of Genesis in the Bible. At the far right, Pharaoh is dreaming of the coming years of plenty and of famine. To the left, Joseph interprets the dream and Pharaoh gives him his ring. In the building in the background, Joseph is reunited with his brothers.

The Metropolitan Museum of Art, New York

many scenes pages 8-9

- 1 nest of baby birds
- 1 hourglass
- 1 peacock
- 1 stormy sea
- 1 pair of porcupines
- 1 bird with its beak in a bottle
- & some playing cards
- & the artist's signature in worms

The Four Continents: Europe, Jan van Kessel

Jan van Kessel shared a love of detailed descriptive nature painting with his grandfather, Jan Bruegel the Elder. Most of Van Kessel's paintings are small and painted on sheets of copper, which provided a perfectly smooth surface for him to work on. In his series portraying four continents, the artist surrounded a central panel with sixteen intimate views: Each of the sixteen in this work is labeled with the name of the city represented.

Alte Pinakothek, Munich

a crowded beach pages 10-11

- 4 baby carriages
- 2 open umbrellas
- 1 shovel in hand
- 2 boys on their backs
- 1 dog on a leash
- 1 trio of cyclists
- 1 signpost
- 2 kings of the hill

July, the Seaside, L. S. Lowry

L. S. Lowry lived near Manchester, England, for most of his life, studying painting in his spare time. He drew scenes of local people in a pocket sketchbook and then painted in his studio at night. Although his career as an artist began to take off after his first London show in 1939, he kept his part-time job as an insurance and rent collector until he was sixty-five. He is well known for his stylized figures of workers and everyday people, and he received the honor of becoming a Royal Academician for his life's work.

Arts Council Collection, Hayward Gallery, London

ancient Egypt page 12

- 1 hare
- 3 cobras
- 1 falcon
- 4 beards
- 10 ears
- 7 hands
- 22 eyes
- 30 feet

Horemhab Offering Wine to Anubis, unknown artist

In ancient Egypt, Anubis, the jackal-headed god, was the lord of the dead and guarded the entombed mummy during the night. Anubis also conducted the "weighing of the heart" ceremony, which determined the fate of the deceased. In this painting from the tomb of King Horemhab, the king is depicted making an offering to Anubis. Horemhab was the last king of the powerful Eighteenth Dynasty, following Akhenaton and Tutankhamen.

The Metropolitan Museum of Art, New York

astronomers page 13

- 1 bull's head
- 2 people writing
- 2 yellow feet
- 2 winged women
- 4 people pointing to the sky
- 1 bridge
- 2 flaming hats
- 3 obelisks

Dionysius the Areopagite Converting the Pagan Philosophers, Antoine Caron

A dramatic solar eclipse that occurred in 1571 may be the subject of this painting. Caron painted it at the court of Catherine de Médicis, queen of France. Eclipses and natural disasters were viewed at that time as foreboding omens. The central figure in the painting, Dionysius the Areopagite, is shown pointing to the sky where a solar eclipse is taking place.

The J. Paul Getty Museum, Los Angeles

India pages 14–15

- 1 musical horse
- 3 pinky rings
- 1 lotus flower
- 1 bull
- 1 flame
- 1 golden eye
- 3 mustaches
- 3 drummers

Vishnu as Varaha, the Cosmic Boar, Slays a Demon General, unknown artist

To fulfill his role as preserver of the universe, the Hindu god Vishnu re-embodies himself in different forms, one of which is Varaha, a white boar. As Varaha, Vishnu saved the world from a demon who tried to drag the earth to the bottom of the ocean. The god is often shown riding his mount, Garuda, the solar bird. Vishnu has four arms and usually carries a conch, a lotus, a club, and a spinning disk, which he has used here to cut off the demon's head.

The Metropolitan Museum of Art, New York

a triumphal procession pages 16–17

- 1 golden bull
- 6 snakes
- 2 goat heads
- 1 horseshoe
- 8 jingle bells
- 4 wings
- 1 lyre
- 1 golden ring

The Entrance of Alexander into Babylon or The Triumph of Alexander, Charles Le Brun

Charles Le Brun was the leading painter in France during the reign of Louis XIV. He is most famous for his murals in the Hall of Mirrors at the palace of Versailles. This painting was the first of four monumental canvases that Le Brun devoted to the history of Alexander the Great. Alexander is shown riding in a chariot pulled by an elephant in his triumphal march into the city of Babylon in 331 B.C.

Louvre Museum, Paris

a Chinese city pages 18-19

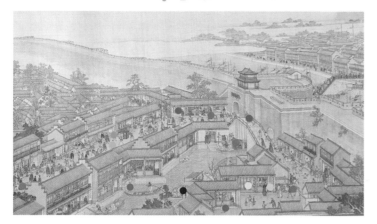

- 1 man trying on boots
- 1 woman with a child
- 1 white beard
- 1 man carrying a flowering branch
- 3 teapots
- 1 fish
- 4 horses
- 1 orange chair

The Qianlong Emperor's Southern Inspection Tour, Scroll Six: Entering Suzhou Along the Grand Canal (detail), Xu Yang

This detail from a handscroll shows a view of the city of Suzhou. The view provides an encyclopedic catalog of daily life in eighteenth-century China, complete with minutely observed descriptions of the shops, residences, and inhabitants of this fabled city. The painter, Xu Yang, had already been a court artist for the emperor Qianlong for twelve years when he began the series of scrolls of the southern inspection tour, which he completed in 1770, in time for the emperor's sixtieth birthday.

The Metropolitan Museum of Art, New York

an Indian battle page 20

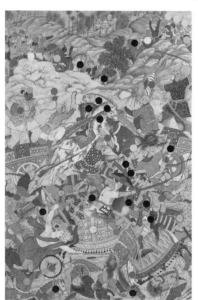

- 2 sets of drums
- 2 elephants
- 17 horses
- 2 golden crowns
- 9 shields
- 3 men with bows
- 1 green boot
- 4 spears

Krishna and Balarama Fight the Enemy, unknown artist

The Mughal emperor Akbar (reign 1556–1605) was fascinated with religion. During his reign, he had a number of Hindu epics translated into the Persian language of the court and illustrated in his workshops. This painting is a page from the *Harivamsa (The Legend of Hari [Krishna])*. The blue-skinned Lord Krishna is shown standing in a chariot and aiming an arrow at the enemy; his brother, Balarama, wears a blue robe and a crown in the foreground and fights using a plow as a weapon.

The Metropolitan Museum of Art, New York

people surrounding a hay wagon page 21

- 2 fish
- 1 peacock feather
- 4 babies
- 2 ladders
- 1 owl
- 5 jugs
- 1 heart
- 1 man growing branches

The Haywain or Path of Life, Hieronymus Bosch

Born into a family of painters, Hieronymus Bosch developed an imaginative style unlike any other artist of his day. His paintings often dealt with religious or moral themes. This painting, the central panel of a triptych, shows people reaching and grabbing for their share of the hay. The wagon is being pulled by demons, giving the painting an ominous feel.

Museo del Prado, Madrid

a fantastic landscape pages 22-23

- 1 owl
- 1 key
- 6 fish
- 1 funnel
- 2 boats
- 1 guitar
- 2 bells
- 1 man on fire

The Temptation of Saint Anthony, follower of Pieter Bruegel the Elder

Pieter Bruegel, the most important artist of the mid–sixteenth century, was known for his mastery of landscape painting. This scene was painted by one of Bruegel's followers, but uses elements, such as the river, from Bruegel's own landscapes and drawings. The fantastic demons in the painting, on the other hand, recall the work of Hieronymus Bosch, another Netherlandish painter whose work was extremely popular in the sixteenth century.

National Gallery of Art, Washington, D.C.

a grand procession pages 24-25

- ○ 5 dogs
- ● 1 hat in hand
- ● 8 birds
- ● 1 pair of red-and-white legs
- ● 1 rabbit
- ● 1 forehead star
- ● 1 hat with writing on the rim
- ○ 9 mustached men

Procession of the Young King, Benozzo Gozzoli

The most important commission that Benozzo Gozzoli received during his long career was to decorate the walls of the chapel in the palace of the Medicis, the ruling family of Florence, Italy, during the Renaissance. The subject of the murals was the journey of the Magi, in which Gozzoli depicted members of the Medici family in sumptuous pageantry.

Medici-Riccardi Palace, Florence

a coronation pages 28-29

- ○ 1 hand without an arm
- ● 2 beards
- ● 1 golden pitcher
- ● 1 hat in hand
- ● 1 golden eagle
- ● 5 winged heads
- ● 1 angel
- ○ 1 sword in hand

Coronation of Emperor Napoléon and Josephine at Notre Dame on December 2, 1804, Jacques-Louis David

Appointed official court painter by Napoléon in 1804, David was given the task of commemorating the emperor's coronation festivities. This canvas depicts the moment when Napoléon crowned his wife Empress, while Pope Pius VII gave his blessing.

Louvre Museum, Paris

children playing pages 26-27

- ○ 1 mask
- ○ 1 wooden flute
- ● 2 red purses
- ● 2 boys on stilts
- ● 1 birdhouse
- ● 2 cone-shaped hats
- ● 1 flower basket
- ○ 1 woman balancing a broom

Children at Play, Pieter Bruegel the Elder

This painter is known as Pieter "the Elder" because one of his sons, also named Pieter, was an artist, too. One of the most universally admired artists in history, Bruegel was a keen observer of common people and village life, and painted everyday scenes with great expression and understanding. In this painting he has portrayed two hundred and thirty children playing ninety different games.

Kunsthistorisches Museum, Vienna

a flat city page 30

- ○ 1 star
- ○ 1 clock
- ● 1 house
- ● 1 apartment building
- ● 1 arrow
- ● 1 blimp
- ● 1 pulley
- ○ & the number 140

Constructive Composition, Joaquín Torres-García

A writer as well as a pioneer of modern painting, Joaquín Torres-García was born in Montevideo, Uruguay. His family moved to Spain in 1891, settling in Barcelona where he studied art and was part of the same artistic circle as the young Pablo Picasso. During a two-year stay in New York in the early 1920s, Torres-García produced paintings of cityscapes in a flat geometric style. He moved to Paris later in that decade, where he developed his own style of constructivist paintings. He returned to Montevideo in 1934.

Solomon R. Guggenheim Museum, New York

a potter at work page 31

- 1 sponge
- 1 funnel
- 9 spouts
- 1 piece of masking tape
- 1 loose-leaf notebook
- 1 spray can
- 1 pot of brushes
- & the number 129

Jeff Kleckner at Work,
Dana Van Horn

Dana Van Horn is a painter and teacher who specializes in the human figure. His subjects have ranged from fellow artists, such as potter Jeff Kleckner, to surfers and political leaders. His large-scale paintings vary from religious murals for churches to portraits for the United States Department of Labor. He teaches painting at Muhlenberg College and at the Baum School of Art, both in Pennsylvania.

The Metropolitan Museum of Art, New York

an alchemist at work pages 32-33

- 1 pair of spectacles
- 1 hourglass
- 4 funnels
- 1 drill
- 1 broken plate
- 1 handwritten note
- 2 baskets
- & the artist's signature

An Alchemist, Adriaen van Ostade

The belief that alchemists could turn base metal into silver and gold lasted until the eighteenth century, and this painting pokes fun at that belief. The piece of paper beside the stool in the painting has an inscription in Latin that reads *oleum et operam perdis* (oil and work is wasted). Alchemists were often accused of losing all of their material possessions to their futile pursuits, as is suggested by this disorderly room.

National Gallery, London

a French harbor pages 34-35

- 5 dogs
- 3 flags
- 1 large white bird
- 1 man with bare feet
- 2 anchors
- 1 guitar case
- 1 waterspout
- & the number 40

The Outer Harbor of Brest, Louis Nicholas van Blarenberghe

Like his father, Jacques-Wilhelm van Blarenberghe (circa 1679–1742), Louis Nicholas initially made his reputation as a painter of battle scenes. Beginning in 1773, he was appointed painter to the Marine Ministry in France and painted a number of views of the port of Brest, of which this is one. A master at depicting crowd scenes, Van Blarenberghe has made the canvas teem with the energy of a busy eighteenth-century port.

The Metropolitan Museum of Art, New York

a large family back cover

- 1 shovel
- 1 wreath
- 3 statues
- 1 jigsaw puzzle
- 2 lion heads
- 1 brass trumpet
- 1 dress without a doll
- 1 horse

The Hatch Family, Eastman Johnson

Painted in 1871, *The Hatch Family* depicts three generations of an American family during the Victorian era in the library of their comfortable Park Avenue house in New York City. Eastman Johnson's portrait is part of the tradition of the "conversation piece," a group portrait with genre details.

The Metropolitan Museum of Art, New York